CONSPIRACY THEORIES
UNBELIEVABLE TRUTHS AND FASCINATING FICTIONS

Published in 2025
First published in the UK by SparkPool Publishing
An imprint of Igloo Books Ltd
Cottage Farm, NN6 0BJ, UK
The authorised representative in the EEA
is Bonnier Books UK (Ireland) Limited.
Registered office address:
Floor 3, Block 3, Miesian Plaza
Dublin 2, D02 Y754, Ireland
compliance@igloobooks.ie
www.igloobooks.com

Copyright © 2025 Igloo Books Ltd

All rights reserved. No part of this publication may be reproduced or transmitted in any form or by any means, electronic, or mechanical, including photocopying, recording, or by any information storage and retrieval system, without permission in writing from the publisher.

1025 001
2 4 6 8 10 9 7 5 3 1
ISBN 978-1-83544-867-0

Illustrated by Alessandro Valdrighi
Written by Gemma Barder
Designed by Simon Parker
Edited by Nicholas Oliver

Printed and manufactured in China

CONTENTS

Introduction 4
Moon Landing 6
The COVID-19 Conspiracy 10
Aliens 14
The Trump Assassination Attempt 18
Flat Earth 22
AI Simulation Theory 26
Cryptozoology 30
Climate Change 34
The 9/11 Attacks 38
The Illuminati 42
MK-Ultra 46
Hollow Earth 50
Havana Syndrome 54
The Disappearance of Agatha Christie 58
The Sinking of the Titanic 62
Geoengineering 66
The Last Flight of Amelia Earhart 70
The Beast of Gévaudan 74
The Vampire of New England 78
Animal Spies 82
The Business Coup Plot 86
The Pendle Swindle 90
Celebrity Body Doubles 94

INTRODUCTION

Did man ever walk on the moon? Did Paul McCartney die in 1966? Is the neighbour's cat obsessed with sunbathing in your garden, or are they actually hiding a secret listening device, recording your every conversation?

Conspiracy theories have been around for as long as people have been able to communicate. Questioning, probing and finding solutions is what makes us human. Whenever there is a strange or shocking event, there will always be an official explanation – and many more theories that question if that explanation is true. From accusing innocent women of being witches in the 1600s, right up to looking at 5G as a cause of the COVID-19 pandemic in 2020, theories can develop from literally anywhere on our planet (and beyond).

Thanks to the increase in communication, first through newspapers and the telephone, then through the internet and social media, we have more information at our fingertips than ever before – and with that information comes more questions to be answered. People are no longer satisfied with accepting one report or one point of view.

When something strange, unexpected or alarming happens, as humans we immediately look for answers. Why did this happen? Who made it happen? How can we stop it happening again? When big businesses, powerful governments or unlawful activities are involved, there's always the belief in some quarters that we are not being told the whole story – but just how much of the story are we missing?

Within this book are some of the most famous conspiracy theories ever to have been proposed (are aliens real?) as well as some that may surprise you (could Beyoncé be part of an international elite determined to take over the world?). Their reach can cover the entire world or focus on the tiniest town. They can involve the most famous people on the planet, or names you might never have heard of. They tell stories that span the last 400 years, proving an enduring desire and resolve to seek the truth and pinpoint accountability, no matter the era.

So, what drives us to look for answers when it appears that we have already been given all the facts? We only have to look at statistics to see that a spike in conspiracy theories usually happens after an unexpected and often tragic event. It took just a few hours after the news broke of the 9/11 attacks in the US for conspiracies to start circulating on the internet. When the famous pilot, Amelia Earhart, went missing in the 1930s, people were desperate for answers, no matter how outlandish they might have been, and when Agatha Christie went missing for 11 days in 1926, the media looked into every possibility behind her disappearance, no matter how unlikely or lacking in evidence some were.

For families and communities who suffered loss hundreds of years ago, a scapegoat was often sought out. Untimely death and failing crops had a huge impact on tightknit societies, so when logic and medicine failed to provide an answer, people turned to the supernatural. Stories of witches, vampires and mythical beasts were considered a certainty. It is easy for anyone with a smartphone to look up a hundred different reasons for why tragedy occurs and to regard our ancestors as misguided, but with all that information could we actually be missing something truly fantastical? Could the supernatural have been silenced with reason?

So, what really is the truth? Each report in this book sets out different points of view surrounding an event or way of thinking. It will discuss the main characters and circumstances that have pushed a conspiracy theory into being and delve into why answers are still being looked for.

Once you have all the information, we'll leave it up to you to decide what you choose to believe, and which conspiracies simply remain… a theory.

MOON LANDING

THE THEORY IN A NUTSHELL

The US's Apollo 11 crew did not land on the moon in 1969, nor on any of the missions that followed. Instead, the famous footage was faked in an attempt to show the world that America had beaten Russia in the Space Race.

THE 1969 MOON LANDING IS arguably the world's most famous conspiracy theory – and for good reason. Despite making household names out of Neil Armstrong and Buzz Aldrin, the belief that the astronauts never made it to the surface of the moon persists. So, why would NASA (National Aeronautics and Space Administration) go to the trouble of faking the moon landing? And what tell-tale signs caused former astronauts and rocket scientists to come out and cry 'hoax'?

NO LANDING CRATER

The Eagle – the lunar landing module of Apollo 11 – touched down on the surface of the moon on 20th July 1969. Shortly after, Neil Armstrong uttered his famous words: 'That's one small step for man, one giant leap for mankind.' However, if we were to look closely at the surface of the moon underneath the Eagle itself, we would see that there is little to no change in the texture of the ground between that area and the rest of the moon. Theorists have argued that if the moon's surface was loose enough for the astronauts to leave footprints, just like fine powder or sand on a beach, surely there should have been some disturbance when the 15-tonne landing module touched down. The theory? The pictures being sent to Earth weren't from the moon at all, but were, in fact, a previously shot and cleverly made film created in Area 51 – the US's top secret base in Nevada.

THE FLYING FLAG

One of the biggest pieces of evidence to suggest that the moon landing was faked, was the triumphant fluttering US flag that was placed when Armstrong and Aldrin stepped onto the moon. However, the moon has no atmosphere, and therefore no wind. So, how was the flag able to fly so proudly? NASA explained this in the early 1990s by saying that there was a rod placed along the length of the flag to keep it extended, and the rippling effect was due to the astronauts having trouble inserting the rod fully into the moon's surface. However, some sceptics believe the footage of the flag being planted clearly shows the flag moving and rippling unaided before the rod was put into place.

STARRY NIGHT... NOT SO MUCH

One thing we can all agree on, whether you believe in this conspiracy or not, is that space is filled with billions of shining stars. Unfortunately, none of the footage taken on 20th July 1969 shows a single star in the pitch-black sky. NASA says that the surface of the moon was so bright that the camera could not pick up the stars, but could this be their way of covering up a glaring misstep by these supposed Nevada filmmakers?

NONE OF THE FOOTAGE TAKEN ON 20TH JULY 1969 SHOWS A SINGLE STAR IN THE PITCH-BLACK SKY.

WHAT WAS IT FOR?

To create a plausible-looking moon landing on a film set would have taken a lot of money, time and the secrecy of hundreds of people. So, why bother? Why did the US desperately want to be seen as the first to reach the moon? Simple: political power. Before Apollo 11 took flight, the US had been locked in the Cold War with the Soviet Union for over two decades. Suspicion and paranoia were at a dangerous level between the two superpowers, and space exploration was high on both of their agendas.

In 1957, the Soviet space program launched a satellite called Sputnik into orbit. It sent shockwaves around the US, leaving them firmly in second place in the Space Race and causing many people to fear that the Soviet Union might put a rocket launcher on the moon ahead of them. Whichever country landed a man on the moon first would not only win bragging rights, but would also show their enemies that they had superior technology and power.

This is the type of camera used by the astronauts to record their time on the moon's surface.

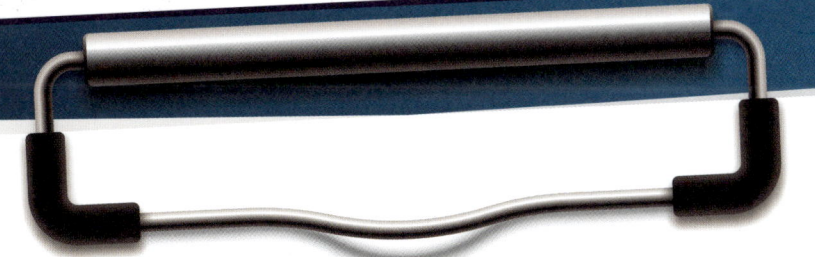

NASA'S RESPONSE

NASA seems to have an explanation for every reason why people think the moon landing was faked, but that has not stopped an estimated 10 per cent of Americans (roughly 34 million people) from still believing the theory. Despite no human having set foot on the moon in over 50 years (if ever), NASA continues to explore the mysteries of the galaxy, as well as sending astronauts to the International Space Station, and on missions to study Mars, Venus and beyond.

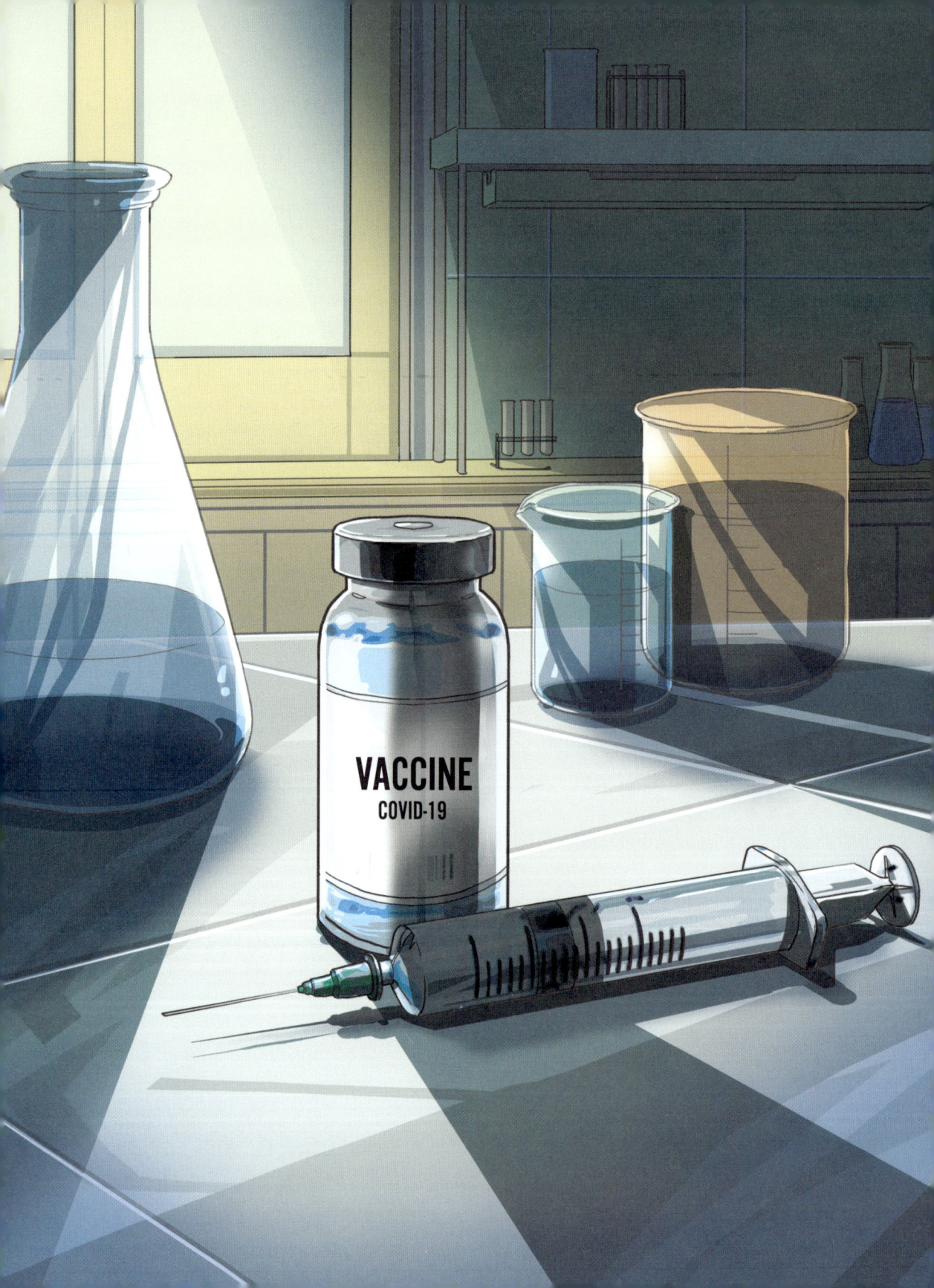

THE COVID-19 CONSPIRACY

THE THEORY IN A NUTSHELL
The COVID-19 pandemic was a man-made virus deliberately unleashed into the world to control countries and their populations.

IN 2020, THE WORLD STOOD still while the SARS-CoV-2 (COVID-19) virus spread across the planet. Schools, offices and shops were closed, and people were asked to stay home. When it looked like the virus could not be stopped, development of a vaccination began. However, along with the virus, conspiracy theories began to spread – not only about the virus itself, but the vaccinations that were being developed to tackle it.

MAN-MADE MENACE?

From the very beginning of the pandemic, we were told that the COVID-19 outbreak likely originated from a seafood and animal market. People in direct contact with the market were taken to hospital with an unknown flu. Certain animals, such as the common raccoon dogs that were sold at the market, were also known to carry COVID-19. For a long time, this is what most people accepted to be the truth. However, it was revealed later on that in the same area as the market was a laboratory specialising in virology – a place that also just happened to have a long history of studying – you guessed it – viruses like COVID-19. Whether the virus came from a market or a laboratory or somewhere else entirely is still very much in debate – however, those who believe the virus was lab-born have used this as evidence for some much darker theories.

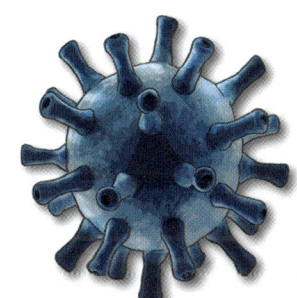

A COVID-19 particle

A WEAPON OF MASS DESTRUCTION

As soon as word spread that the virus could have been leaked from a laboratory, conspiracy theories started to circulate online that suggested COVID-19 was developed as a result of research into biological weapons. Nations clashed as prominent US politicians began referring to COVID-19 as the 'China virus', whereas China began calling it the 'America virus'.

Whatever COVID-19's origins, the arguing between two world superpowers fuelled the belief that COVID-19 was a man-made weapon, specifically designed to cause maximum harm.

VACCINATION CONTROL

Whatever the origin, for whatever the reason, the COVID-19 pandemic was causing millions of deaths across the world and had to be contained. The best way to do this was to practise social distancing and to get the majority of the population vaccinated. However, not everyone was convinced that the vaccination being rolled out was entirely for the good of the world.

'Anti-vaxxers' had a variety of reasons for going against the vaccination rollout. Some suggested that the vaccines were a cover for large pharmaceutical companies (Big Pharma) to make money, or that COVID-19 was not as serious as we were being told. Another group found evidence that Bill Gates – the billionaire CEO of Microsoft – had predicted the pandemic back in 2015 when he delivered a TED talk. He warned that the world was not ready for a worldwide viral outbreak, and that we should be investing more time and energy into stopping it from happening. From this, a theory sprouted that Gates was somehow 'in' on the pandemic. He wanted to use the vaccination programmes as a way of tracking and controlling the population. How? By placing a microchip into each dose of the vaccine.

THE SPREAD OF 5G

Before the pandemic took hold, a new generation of wireless technology was being rolled out across the world. 5G was going to make communication faster and more reliable. However, the timing of this new development alongside the COVID-19 outbreak was too much of a coincidence for some. The theory suggested that the waves emitted from the 5G towers were weakening immune systems, making people more susceptible to flu-like viruses, and some went as far as to say they were spreading the virus. The theory was so well believed that some 5G masts were set on fire in Birmingham and Liverpool in the UK just a month after the country went into its first lockdown.

THE PANDEMIC CAUSED MILLIONS OF DEATHS ACROSS THE WORLD.

A TESTING TIME

The COVID-19 pandemic was a frightening time for everyone across the globe. When people are scared, they tend to look for explanations – no matter where they come from – and this is perhaps why so many conspiracy theories have emerged. When teamed with the fact that even world leaders can't seem to agree on what happened and why, it is no wonder that one of the strangest events in recent history is still widely disputed. While investigations are still taking place, and the world is in recovery, there are plenty of unanswered questions that we need to find the answers to – if we ever can.

ALIENS

THE THEORY IN A NUTSHELL
Extraterrestrial lifeforms are real and have visited Earth, sometimes making contact with the most unlikely people.

ALIEN, A QUIET PLACE, Arrival, Men in Black, Independence Day... it feels like we just can't stop telling stories about what might be living out there among the stars. While there are thousands of books and films about extra-terrestrials, what is the truth? More importantly, what are we not being told?

AREA 51

Area 51 is a huge, very secretive US Air Force facility in southern Nevada. A place that is surrounded by mystery, the approximately 38,000-acre base has become so intertwined with stories of UFOs and alien life forms, that the area itself has become a hotbed of rumour and gossip.

To understand the fuss, we must look at what drew the world's attention to the facility in the first place. Although the US still claims that Area 51 is an Air Force development and testing facility, it has been the location of numerous UFO sightings and a former employee even came out in the 1980s to claim that he worked on 'non-human technology'.

So why there? According to some theories, it all began in 1947...

THE ROSWELL INCIDENT

In 1947, headlines were made across the globe when the US military declared it was in the possession of an unidentified 'flying disc' that had crash-landed in Roswell, New Mexico. Excitement grew as the world believed they finally had proof that alien life existed. Strangely, just a few days later, the story was retracted, and a far less exciting explanation was given. The 'disc' was simply part of a crashed weather balloon, and nothing other-worldly at all. Over 75 years later, people still aren't buying it.

In fact, it is widely believed that the debris from the Roswell crash, including an alien ship and deceased alien life forms, were taken to Area 51 to be studied and kept away from the public eye – and that is where they remain to this day.

ALIEN ABDUCTION

For as long as UFOs have captured the world's imagination, there have been stories of people being taken aboard alien spacecraft. Some stories are more believable than others, but one tale by Terry Lovelace, a retired assistant attorney general in Vermont, US, rings truer than most. Lovelace, who kept his story secret for over 40 years, was camping with a friend when a gigantic floating pyramid came towards them. The pyramid seemed to scan their bodies before both men started to feel sleepy.

When Lovelace awoke, he saw a group of children in the meadow behind their camp. When he asked his friend what a group of children were doing in the campsite in the middle of the night, Lovelace's friend replied: 'They aren't little kids. Don't you remember they took us and they hurt us?' Lovelace then began to piece together what happened when he was taken aboard the alien ship, and in the years that followed he had hypnotherapy to remember more.

An interpretation of what the 'flying disc' that crash-landed in Roswell may have looked like.

MR GODFREY'S STORY

Similar stories from men and women who had no previous interest in aliens or UFOs can be found all over the world, including police officer Alan Godfrey. Now a pensioner, Godfrey became a reluctant local celebrity in 1980 when he came face-to-face with a floating diamond-shaped object in Yorkshire in the UK. Godfrey awoke around 30 minutes after seeing this UFO, 27 m down the road from where he had originally been, with no initial memory of what had happened. Later on, however, Godfrey recalled that during the half an hour he was 'out', he believed he had woken up inside a room and was being examined by 'small beings'.

IT IS WIDELY BELIEVED THAT THE DEBRIS FROM THE ROSWELL CRASH WAS TAKEN TO AREA 51.

POLITICAL POWER

UFOs, aliens and abductions often feel like the stuff of fiction. However, as space exploration grows and our knowledge of the universe increases, governments worldwide seem to be taking things a little more seriously.

In 2007, the Pentagon admitted it was studying UFOs and set up the Advanced Aerospace Threat Identification Program (AATIP) for this very reason. President Barack Obama went on record to say that he had seen footage of aircraft that no one could explain, and Nick Pope, a former UFO investigator for the Ministry of Defence, thinks that stories like Terry Lovelace's and Alan Godfrey's could, in fact, be genuine.

THE TRUMP ASSASSINATION ATTEMPT

THE THEORY IN A NUTSHELL

The assassination attempt on the (then former) President of the United States, Donald Trump, was staged.

ON THE EVENING OF 13th July 2024, Donald Trump took to the stage for a Republican rally at Butler Farm Show Grounds in Pennsylvania. A few minutes into his speech, shots were fired – and it appeared that Trump had been hit.

THE IMMEDIATE AFTERMATH

Tragically, a member of the crowd who had come to support Trump was killed, with two more critically injured. Security services were able to disable the gunman, who was also killed. Trump was taken to a local hospital for treatment but came away with just a wound on his ear.

Within minutes, news of Trump's attempted assassination – including iconic images of the event – was spread over social media, and it was not long before people on both sides of the political spectrum were beginning to question whether everything was as it seemed.

BY ORDER OF THE DEMOCRATS

Donald Trump became president of the United States for the first time in 2016 and is one of the most divisive politicians the US has ever seen. His controversial statements and actions are both hated and loved by millions of Americans. What cannot be denied, however, is his popularity. In 2020, he failed to be reelected, beaten by Joe Biden. But in July 2024, Trump was firmly back on the campaign trail, drumming up support for a second term in office. Knowing the threat Trump posed, did the Democrats plan something drastic? A quote from Joe Biden, taken from a private call to his National Finance Committee, reads: 'We're done talking about the debate. It's time to put Trump in the bullseye.'

Soon Trump began to add fuel to the theory. 'It's very suspicious,' Trump said when interviewed about the event on a podcast later in the year. 'The more you see it, the more you start to say, "There could be something else".' After Biden stepped down due to intraparty battles, Trump faced Kamala Harris and went on to win a second term as president in 2024.

BY ORDER OF THE REPUBLICANS

No, we don't mean that there were people in Donald Trump's own party who wanted him dead. Rather, that the former president and his team came up with the idea of a faked assassination attempt to paint Trump as a hero. Evidence for this theory soon mounted up. Pictures circulated on social media, taken moments after the assassination attempt, that show Trump and his security guards smiling as they 'pretended' to cover the president from a further attack – although it was widely believed these images had been manipulated using AI.

Social media users also questioned how Trump was able to stand up so quickly and pose for the cameras with blood streaming down his face. The photo soon became so popular among Trump's supporters that it was emblazoned on everything from T-shirts to mugs.

One crucial piece of evidence that both sides believed would prove their theory was suspiciously kept out of the press coverage; details of the medical care Trump received when he was taken to Butler Memorial Hospital have never been released.

THE SHOOTER

Police records show that 20-year-old Thomas Matthew Crooks was the shooter on that fateful day in July. Trump's security team was alerted to the fact that a young man was on the roof of a nearby building, but it was too late to stop Crooks from taking his shot. Just a few seconds after the assassination attempt, Crooks was shot dead. But how was a young man allowed to get such a clear shot at the former president? The building had a clear line of sight to Trump's podium but, strangely, was outside the security perimeter patrolled by Trump's team. Crooks was able to climb onto the roof with his gun, an AR-15 rifle, and shoot eight rounds of bullets towards Trump before being stopped. When his car was found, there were explosives inside – suggesting Crooks was planning an even bigger attack. These mistakes led to an investigation into the Secret Service, where the press found that Director Kimberly Cheatle was unable to answer their questions. Investigations into Crooks showed he had supported both the Republicans and Democrats in the past – so could he have been a willing participant for either side's scheme?

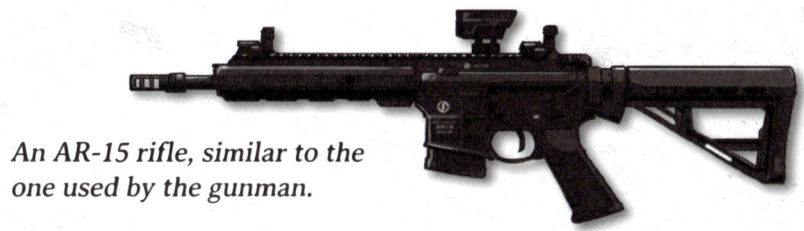

An AR-15 rifle, similar to the one used by the gunman.

FACTS AND FEELINGS

An assassination attempt by scared Democrats? A piece of staged propaganda by the Republicans? Or simply a series of mistakes made by the Secret Service that allowed a shooter clear access to the former president? Whatever truly happened on that day, we can say one thing for certain; most people have an opinion on Donald Trump and those opinions can often be extreme. At moments like these, as well as studying the evidence, supposed or otherwise, we should also consider how our personal opinions can alter the way we look at the facts.

FLAT EARTH

THE THEORY IN A NUTSHELL

The Earth is flat, and governments and organisations are colluding with each other to keep the truth from the wider public.

THE EARTH IS ROUND.
The facts are overwhelming, right? Scientific, mathematic, photographic – the quantity of verified, established evidence is staggering. And yet, there are people today who fervently believe that the Earth is flat. Sceptical of science and the mainstream media, flat-earthers have turned a blind eye to the evidence and hold stringently to their own beliefs.

FROM SPHERE TO ETERNITY

Around 330 BCE, Greek polymath Aristotle observed that only a spherical Earth would make the circular shadow projected onto the Moon during a lunar eclipse. The shadow remained circular no matter where the Sun was positioned in the sky. He also proved the curvature of the horizon by noting that the hull of a ship would disappear over the horizon first – something only possible on a spherical planet. If the Earth was flat, the whole ship would remain visible as it sailed off into the distance.

You'd think this would put the matter to bed, but let's jump ahead to 19th-century England. More specifically, to 1838 at Old Bedford River, Cambridgeshire. Here, Samuel Rowbotham, an early exponent of the flat earth theory and author of *Zetetic Astronomy: Earth Not a Globe*, conducted what is known as the 'Bedford Level Experiment'. He claimed the experiment proved the Earth was flat as the boats he watched through a telescope never dipped below the horizon. But what he hadn't accounted for was light refraction, which scientists later discovered when attempting the experiment for themselves. Despite this debunking of Rowbotham's findings, flat-earthers still claim to this day what he discovered was correct.

A bust of Aristotle.

THE ICE WALL THEORY

It was the internet that gave flat-earthers a space to come together and share research on different theories. There isn't one single theory which flat-earthers agree on, but two theories in particular have captured the imagination.

One theory claims that the Earth is flat, shaped like a circle and bordered by an ice wall – imagine a giant Petri dish. This wall is estimated to be around 45 m high and several hundred metres thick.

Is there evidence to support this? Well, certainly no scientific evidence. But when you're a science-sceptic, you're prepared to look elsewhere for your information. Take the Antarctic Treaty of 1959, for example. It was signed by twelve countries who all agreed Antarctica would be used only for peaceful purposes such as scientific research. But some flat-earthers theorise that it was instead a global agreement whereby the countries involved would use their military power to prevent anyone from travelling to the planet's edge and discovering the truth for themselves.

HIDDEN IN PLAIN SIGHT

Even though flat-earthers claim government interference prevents them from proving the ice wall theory correct, some believe evidence of this global conspiracy has been hiding in plain sight. Take a look at the United Nations flag: conspiracy theorists claim this flag matches their view of what a flat earth looks like almost exactly, with the olive branches as a nod to the ice wall.

UNDER THE DOME

Other flat-earthers claim that the planet is underneath a huge dome, with the Moon and Sun also inside, circling the Earth's surface to give the effect of day and night – the Sun acting as a sort of spotlight. This dome theory would make space travel impossible, and indeed some believe the purpose of NASA is to push the false narrative that the Earth is spherical.

The 'Blue Marble' photo taken in 2012 is an example of photo manipulation flat-earthers believe NASA has been using to push their own agenda onto the masses. This is a picture of the planet taken from the VIIRS instrument aboard the NASA satellite 'Suomi NPP'. Flat-earthers claim it is clear to see where the lighting is different and where certain areas don't line up correctly. And they're absolutely right. But it's not what they think. The photo is actually a composite of several smaller photos of the planet taken in low orbit. It has to be pieced together this way as NASA claims it's impossible to take several photos of the Earth and keep the lighting, cloud formations and so on, exactly the same within each photograph.

> A GROUP OF PEOPLE BELIEVE THE EARTH IS FLAT, SHAPED LIKE A CIRCLE AND BORDERED BY AN ICE WALL.

AROUND IN CIRCLES

Believers and non-believers alike are fascinated by the flat earth theory, but for very different reasons. The 'globesters' wonder how people can ignore a stack of proof backed by science, photographs and so on, and the flat-earthers can't understand why people so freely believe the information presented to them by government organisations and the mainstream media. What's for certain is that it's highly unlikely the two opposing groups will ever find common ground.

AI SIMULATION THEORY

THE THEORY IN A NUTSHELL

Our lived reality is actually a computer simulation and we are being controlled by a higher being or highly developed Artificial Intelligence (AI).

IF YOU HAVE NEVER HEARD OF the AI Simulation Theory, the easiest way to explain it is to put this book down, watch *The Matrix* (1999), then come back to us. As well as being entertained by Keanu Reeves for over two hours, you will also have a basic understanding of what AI simulation means. In its simplest terms, AI simulation theorists believe that all human consciousness is being controlled by a computer system. We are, in fact, avatars in a giant computer game.

SIMULATION IS NOW

In 2003, Swedish philosopher Nick Bostrom wrote a paper called *Are You Living in a Computer Simulation?* In it, he argues that humans today are not living and breathing creatures, but rather that our consciousness is being controlled by an advanced human race, perhaps thousands of years into the future. In effect, we are living in a virtual world. The humans we believe we are, are actually historic versions of the 'real' humans who control us. What we believe to be our world is a giant computer programme, being controlled by a future version of the human race who are far cleverer than us! Even the creation of this very book would be classed as gameplay in the simulation.

Some proof that this could be possible was provided by OpenWorm, a project dedicated in part to creating an artificial simulation of the behaviours of a roundworm within a computer. The theory argued by some is that, as research into AI grows, the same technology applied to the worm could be used to replicate human behaviour, too, assuming it isn't already...

THE THEORY IS HUNDREDS OF YEARS OLD

It is easy to think that the AI Simulation Theory is a very recent creation. Electronic computers have only been around for the past 80 years and the technology for AI is relatively new in comparison. However, the French philosopher René Descartes, born over 400 years ago in 1596, was actually one of the first people to seriously question what 'reality' really is – and whether the truth of our reality, really is the truth. Descartes posed the question: What if my mind is being manipulated into seeing, thinking and feeling the things that I do? For example, is the grass green or is something (or someone) manipulating me into thinking that it is? Is this apple sweet, or am I being told what 'sweet' is?

Descartes said the only thing we can believe in is what we think, but the world outside of our own minds is unknowable. If Descartes' theory were true, then it is not too much of a leap to say that the only thing we can trust is our own mind, and that everything else might be being controlled by outside forces.

THE SIMS TAKEOVER

David Chalmers is a professor of Philosophy at New York University, and he takes the video game *The Sims* very seriously. In *The Sims*, players get to create their own world and control human characters in real-life situations. Sims can get married, have children, build a career and even get ill and pass away. Within one game there can be multiple generations of a family and millions of different scenarios. Chalmers argues that a game like *The Sims* already has millions of simulated people and that one day the technology will be so advanced that these simulated people will outnumber the amount of real people on the planet (if it doesn't already).

If we look at the statistics between the amount of simulated people in the world, and the amount of 'real' people, Chalmers says that the odds are that we are the simulated ones!

PHILOSOPHY VS REALITY

Whether you are a fan of technology, sci-fi or video games, the AI Simulation Theory is one of the most interesting debates currently being discussed. With highly-educated minds seriously considering the idea that our world is computer-generated, we may soon see the theory stepping out of the shadows of conspiracy and into the light of the mainstream. However, one big problem still hovers over every facet of this theory, whether it comes from an academic viewpoint or not. There is no way of proving if our reality is true or controlled.

For example, Person A says that their reality is not being controlled, but Person B says that they could be being controlled into saying that! Person B says that they are being controlled, but Person A wants to see evidence, which, of course, Person B cannot provide unless told to do so while being controlled. It is a deadlock that is sure to be unpicked for many years to come!

As AI technology continues to grow at an astonishing rate, might computer chips such as this become a part of us?

WHAT IF YOUR MIND IS BEING MANIPULATED INTO SEEING, THINKING AND FEELING THE THINGS THAT YOU DO?

CRYPTOZOOLOGY

THE THEORY IN A NUTSHELL
Creatures that were once thought to be extinct, or the subject of myths and legends, really do exist.

GIANT SHARKS, HALF-HUMAN creatures and sea monsters all seem to be the stuff of legend (and nightmares). However, the stories around the existence of creatures such as megalodon, Bigfoot and the Loch Ness monster continue to fascinate. Cryptozoologists study the evidence and champion the idea that these 'cryptids' really are part of our world.

MEGA MEGALODON

Megalodon was a giant prehistoric shark that stalked the oceans of the world during the Miocene and Pliocene epochs – between 23 and 3 million years ago. Fossils of, and teeth from, the mackerel shark (thought to have been up to 24 m long) have been found on every continent in the world, except Antarctica. The gigantic beast is most closely related to mako sharks, and is thought to have been one of the biggest predators to have ever existed. So, why do cryptozoologists have their eye on the megalodon today, when most archaeologists agree that it became extinct millions of years ago?

A growing pile of visual evidence, theories that a megalodon has been captured and the mysteries that still surround some unexplored areas of the ocean, have opened up the possibility that megalodon did not die out at all. An image that was circulated on social media in 2024 shows a black and white photograph of a captured megalodon in front of a ship, dated from the 1900s. While many people claimed the image was AI-generated, for some it showed proof that megalodon isn't extinct.

CAGED CREATURE

In 2024, a series of TikTok videos were trending, all seeming to point to the discovery of a huge underwater cage, owned by NASA, that contained a megalodon. George Meyer, a scientist studying marine animals, reported that he had been blown off course by a storm and when the waters settled, he saw the cage beneath him. He dived down to explore and was allegedly confronted by the gigantic creature. However, when he later returned, he was unable to locate the cage or the shark.

BIGFOOT

Bigfoot – or Sasquatch, as it is sometimes known – is believed to be a giant, human-like creature who makes its home in the forests of North America. The legend of Bigfoot has been popular in the US and Canada for over a hundred years, but it wasn't until 1958 that it was given the name 'Bigfoot'. An employee of a logging company found a set of 16-inch-long footprints in the mud in Humboldt County, California, that looked as though they had been made by a human or ape-like foot. This, along with other strange incidents, such as heavy equipment being moved without explanation, led to a local news story of the giant wildman living in the woods.

In 1967, Roger Patterson and Bob Gimlin shot what has become the most-famous footage of Bigfoot. They captured the roaming, fur-covered man in the woods of northern California, and their footage has been debated ever since. In the video, a non-human creature can clearly be seen striding across the screen before glancing back at the camera. Although Patterson passed away in 1972, he remained resolute that the film was real. Gimlin did not talk about the film very often, though in 2005 he began to attend Bigfoot events and talk about what he saw.

Bigfoot

THE LOCH NESS MONSTER

For 1500 years, stories of a 'water beast' have surrounded the beautiful Loch Ness in the Scottish Highlands. This mythical creature still fascinates tourists today, with the Loch Ness Centre attracting 1.6 million visitors a year. But what exactly is the 'monster' lurking in the waters of Loch Ness, and how could it have survived for so long? Numerous investigations have taken place over the years, some official and some less so, which have reported various findings. A sample of water taken from the loch suggested 'Nessie' could be a form of giant eel, while other investigations used sonar to look for large mammals living underwater.

By far the most compelling evidence for the Loch Ness monster comes from the huge amount of anecdotal and photographic evidence that has been collected over the years. It was in 1934 that the story of Nessie truly captured the world's imagination, when three sightings of a 'dragon or prehistoric monster' were reported within a short space of time. Despite the excitement and romanticisation of the Loch Ness monster, there have been professional investigations into what the creature might be. The most common explanation is that it is a form of plesiosaur that has somehow survived millions of years after the rest of its kind became extinct, thanks to the unique and deep waters of Loch Ness.

THEORY: NASA IS KEEPING A MEGALODON IN A GIANT CAGE AT THE BOTTOM OF THE OCEAN.

JUST HAVEN'T MET YOU YET

Nearly all countries and societies in the world seem to have their own cryptids, such as El Chupacabra, the strange vampire-like creature from the Latin Americas, and Mokele-mbembe, the water-dwelling dinosaur from the Congo Basin in Central Africa. Add to this the fact that so much of our planet is still yet to be explored, and the idea that some of these strange creatures might actually exist does not seem so unbelievable after all.

CLIMATE CHANGE

THE THEORY IN A NUTSHELL

Climate change is not real and is being used to control our actions, while big companies look to keep their profits healthy.

WHEREVER THERE IS POLITICAL debate or an election to be won, the discussion of climate change is always high on the agenda. However, not everyone on the political spectrum, or within the general public, can agree on why our climate is changing – or even if it is changing at all.

ARE WE THE PROBLEM?

Most environmental studies and eco-activists agree that the main cause of climate change is simple: humans. The planet has existed for over 4.5 billion years, however 95 per cent of what causes climate change has been attributed to modern humans.

The food we eat, the way we travel and how we dispose of our waste increases the level of CO_2 in our air that causes the Earth to heat up. Since 1982, the rate of warming has increased three times as much as it did between 1950 and 1982. Leading ecological experts agree that the Earth will continue to heat up unless something dramatic changes.

PIERS CORBYN

In 2019, astrophysicist Piers Corbyn had a different point of view. During a debate at Reading University in the UK, he argued that it is not humans causing CO2 levels to rise, but other natural factors. Corbyn says that only 4 per cent of CO2 is affected by man, so what about the other 96 per cent? He believes that it is plant growth and decay – and even methane created by termites – that is a far bigger problem than air travel or intensive farming. Academics argued back, asking: if this were true, why would leading politicians and activists be so concerned about changing the way we live in order to stop global warming?

Corbyn, and a growing number of his peers, believe the answer is simple. The warnings over the harm we are causing to the environment are just a way for the government to increase tax on certain items and create more control over public behaviour.

WHO'S BEHIND THE RESEARCH?

The CO2 Coalition is a think tank that aims to promote the idea that CO2 is actually *helping* the planet. Set up in 2015, it received thousands of dollars in charitable donations from some pretty influential people and claims to '… shift the debate from the unjustified criticism of CO2 and fossil fuels to one based on a solid scientific foundation'. Any research into the effects of CO2 was welcomed by environmentalists and campaigners alike, but it was soon discovered that the Coalition was largely funded by fossil fuel companies – the very companies being blamed for the increase.

Despite the compelling arguments the Coalition put across, we must wonder how unbiased the findings were. It reminded some people of the 'research' conducted by American tobacco companies in the 1960s and 70s, persuading the public that smoking wasn't as harmful as it actually was and it could also be good for mental health!

THE CO2 COALITION WAS LARGELY FUNDED BY FOSSIL FUEL COMPANIES.

POLAR ICE CAPS

Rising sea levels are often cited as one of the clear indicators of global warming, with polar ice caps melting and adding water to the ocean. However, a meme from 2022, which went viral in 2024, aimed to prove that this area of thinking was wrong, and at worst, a hoax by environmentalists to further their agenda. The meme shows a jug of water with ice cubes floating in it. As the ice cubes melt, the volume of the water in the jug does not increase. This simple science experiment aimed to show that melting ice caps would not increase sea levels. However, experts retaliated by stating that the rising sea levels were not due to ice already in the water, but rather land-based ice that falls into the ocean when it melts and breaks away.

Similarly, in 2015, journalist James Taylor wrote an article for *Forbes* (later removed for failing to meet the magazine's editorial standards) claiming he had found evidence that the polar ice caps were not melting. In it, he shows data from NASA that tracks trends in polar sea ice. The data showed no difference, and even some improvement, to sea ice levels since 1979. Again, however, Taylor was missing the big picture; sea ice is not the problem, the huge sheets of land ice that are melting and falling into the sea are.

Polar bears are just one of the many animals affected by climate change.

AN INTERNATIONAL PROBLEM

In 2024, nearly 200 countries attended the COP29 Climate Change Conference in Baku, Azerbaijan. The aim of the conference was to make sure all countries were dedicated to helping tackle climate change, especially in developing countries. However, questions were raised as to whether the conference was purely just for show, and that the deals they made were influenced by, or watered down to appease, fossil fuel companies. With both sides of the theory using each fresh news story and natural disaster as further proof of their own ideas, it seems the climate change discussion is set to rumble on for many years to come.

THE 9/11 ATTACKS

THE THEORY IN A NUTSHELL

The attacks on the US conducted by al-Qaeda on 11th September 2001 were previously known about, or even orchestrated by, the US government.

SHOCKWAVES WERE FELT across the world on 11th September 2001, when two passenger aeroplanes were flown into the World Trade Center office buildings in New York, US. A third plane destroyed the western face of the Pentagon - the giant headquarters of the US military. A fourth plane crashed in a field in Pennsylvania after passengers fought back. It is thought the hijackers had meant to attack Washington's Capitol Building.

TERRORIST ATTACK

What at first looked like a tragic accident was later confirmed to be a terrorist attack by al-Qaeda, a pan-Islamist militant organisation. While the world came to terms with the deaths of 2977 people, and what this attack on the US meant for international politics, theories started to emerge over what we were being told – or not being told – about these tragic events.

A Boeing 767 – the same make of plane which hit the World Trade Center.

PLANNING FOR WAR

On the morning of 11th September 2001, the 43rd President of the United States, George W. Bush, was on his way to the Emma E. Booker Elementary School in Florida to read with children. It was supposed to be a photo opportunity to show how invested the administration was in education. However, on the way to the school, the president was informed that a plane had hit one of the World Trade Center buildings. Despite some of his advisors immediately recognising that it was a terrorist attack, Bush simply asked if the weather was bad in New York. Frances Townsend, Director of the Office of International Programs for the Department of Justice, knew that the planes had been deliberately flown into the towers. Her experience told her that any commercial jet pilot would have done anything they could to avoid hitting the buildings. Despite this, Bush continued with his visit. He took a seat at the front of the classroom and casually flipped through a copy of *The Pet Goat*. When the second plane hit, Andrew Card, White House chief of staff, whispered in the president's ear that the US was under attack. Again, Bush seemed calm and went back to his book.

When the president and his team finally pulled themselves together to make a statement to the press, Bush seemed casual. He referred to the terrorists as 'those folks' and then, tellingly, he ended with the words 'this will not stand'. The words were identical to comments made by his father, the 41st President of the United States, George H. W. Bush, before the US entered the Gulf War. Conspiracy theorists believed this was proof that Bush had already made plans to go to war and that his administration was behind the attacks that would start one.

As well as Bush's immediate response to the attack, misinformation and theories of cover-ups continued to plague the event. The BBC (British Broadcasting Corporation) released the names of 19 hijackers thought to have died during the attack, but it was later discovered that all 19 were alive. In addition to this, the planes' black boxes, which could have provided key information about the last moments of the fated planes, were not all recovered.

EVEN AFTER HE WAS INFORMED ABOUT THE SECOND PLANE HITTING, BUSH SEEMED CALM AND WENT BACK TO HIS BOOK.

DID THE US GOVERNMENT KNOW?

George W. Bush, had only been in office for eight months by the time the 9/11 attacks took place. Although he was seen as a divisive choice, and sometimes mocked for his unusual choice of words, Bush was keen to step out of the shadow of his father and make his mark on the world. It was commonly known that George W. Bush and his administration wanted to take on Saddam Hussein, the Iraqi dictator, but he did not have an argument strong enough to take his country to war. For this reason, some theorists believe that when the US government was given information that an attack on the US was going to happen, they decided it would be the perfect way to strengthen their argument.

These theories don't provide any evidence as to whether George W. Bush and his team knew how catastrophic the damage would be, or if they thought they could stop it before tragedy struck. What is known is that one of the masterminds behind the tragedy, Zacarias Moussaoui, was already well-known to the FBI, but his home was never searched. A former FBI agent, Coleen Rowley, was so shocked at this lack of investigation into Moussaoui that she wrote to the director of the FBI to express her concerns. Some theories suggest that if Moussaoui had been investigated, they would have discovered evidence of the 9/11 plot in his home – and potentially stopped the attacks.

POLITICAL POWER

In July 2004, the *Final Report of the National Commission on Terrorist Attacks Upon the United States* was released. Nearly three years after the attacks, the report aimed to give grieving relatives and official bodies a full account of what happened. This official report exposed failures within the FBI and intelligence services as well as a lack of coordination between government departments in the immediate aftermath of the event. However, instead of putting to bed the doubts and suspicions of what led to the deaths of so many people, it raised further questions for theorists as to what truly happened on that fateful day, and during the months leading up to it.

THE ILLUMINATI

THE THEORY IN A NUTSHELL

There is an elite and highly secretive group of people called the Illuminati. Above politics, royalty and religion, their aim is to create a 'new world order' controlling the planet without detection.

IN 1776, A PROFESSOR OF LAW at the University of Ingolstadt in Bavaria decided to set up a secret society. Adam Weishaupt was fed up with royalty and religion dictating how society should think and behave, and he decided that he and his friends could do a better job! The Order of the Illuminati was formed and grew to have around 1500 members by 1780. In 1785, the Duke of Bavaria outlawed the group – and any secret society like it. However, rumours of the Illuminati still exist, with celebrity names often attached.

A 1960s RESURGENCE

Despite being outlawed nearly 200 years earlier, the Illuminati theory really started to gain popularity again in the mid-1960s. A booklet called *Principia Discordia* became widely popular and challenged the reader to question the way their life was governed. Was it really politicians and royals who ruled the world, or are we all being lied to? From this booklet, a three-volume novel called *Illuminatus* was written that contained virtually every conspiracy theory ever dreamt of. The book even suggested that Adam Weishaupt killed and replaced George Washington – making the founder of the Illuminati also the founding father of the USA! The books were so popular that they were adapted into a nine-hour play starring British actors Bill Nighy and Jim Broadbent.

THE ALL-SEEING EYE

If you have ever looked at a dollar bill, you might have noticed the eye inside a floating triangle. The eye is known as the 'Eye of Providence' and represents God watching over humanity. It also just so happens to be the symbol of the Illuminati. The eye appears all over the world, in different cultures, religions and societies. It has been used on masonic buildings, churches and religious artwork. So, could this be proof that this elite group really is all around us, and has been for hundreds of years, or simply that an eye within a triangle is so popular that all these different walks of life adopted the same symbol for themselves?

Some conspiracy theorists claim the image of the all-seeing eye above an incomplete pyramid, seen on the back of the US $1 bill, is proof that Freemasonry, or even the Illuminati itself, influenced the founding of the United States.

FROM ROYALS TO RAPPERS

The singer Katy Perry once said that if you are accused of being in the Illuminati, then you have really made it in life! Of course, she also denied being a member of the exclusive group. The list of famous people who are believed to be part of the Illuminati goes as far back as the 3rd US president, Thomas Jefferson, and has even included Queen Elizabeth II.

More recently, names such as Jay-Z, Beyoncé and Taylor Swift have all been linked with the group. Beyoncé is said to have made the Illuminati symbol with her hands during a Super Bowl halftime performance, and former President Joe Biden also talked about creating a 'new world order' in one of his speeches. And it is not simply celebrities and powerful heads of state who are said to be part of the Illuminati. It has long been believed that Illuminati members are placed high up in the Vatican.

THE EYE OF PROVIDENCE IS THE SYMBOL OF THE ILLUMINATI.

THE END GAME

Originally, the goal of the Illuminati was to create an elite group of men who would gradually take over the world – disposing of all religion, monarchies and political parties. If superstars such as Beyoncé and Taylor Swift have been recruited, their intentions must have changed slightly! But does their goal remain the same? Understandably, most celebrities questioned have laughed off the suggestion and, as it stands, the Illuminati as a group (if they exist) remain highly secretive and underground.

MK-ULTRA

THE THEORY IN A NUTSHELL

The almost-unbelievable MK-Ultra experiments were not halted in 1973. Rather, they continue to control the minds of celebrities and murderers.

MIND CONTROL, hallucinogenic drugs, non-consensual human experimentation – unlike many of the reports in this book, the story of MK-Ultra has been proven beyond doubt to be true. From 1953 to 1973, the CIA undertook a series of wild, cruel and strange experiments that were carried out on humans to see if mind control was truly possible. Thankfully, MK-Ultra was shut down and the details of what took place were revealed to the world in 1975.

MIND CONTROL

One of the main aims of the MK-Ultra experiment was to see if it was possible to control a human mind. Some reports say that the CIA was able to achieve a basic level of mind control on a dog, dictating its behaviour using microchips inserted into its brain. From this, one theory has emerged that suggests MK-Ultra developed the technology even further to enable them to control a human brain. So, who better to apply this technology to than those who have incredible reach and power – such as celebrities. Well-known names such as Cardi B, Lady Gaga and even Hillary Clinton have been suspected of being under MK-Ultra's control – suggesting that they have traded their autonomy for success. Footage of Cardi B 'zoning out' while being interviewed and Lady Gaga making strange hand gestures on television have both been attributed to MK-Ultra 'glitches'.

The theory also goes as far to say that some of the numerous shootings happening on a daily basis in the US can be blamed on gunmen being controlled by MK-Ultra technology used by terrorist organisations, or to push political agendas.

JONESTOWN MASSACRE

Just five years after MK-Ultra was supposedly shut down, one of the most notorious and tragic massacres took place on a commune called 'Jonestown' in Guyana, South America. Jonestown was a settlement for the fundamental religious cult known as the Peoples Temple, headed by Jim Jones. The Christian cult had moved its members from the US to the settlement in Guyana after an article was published exposing the abuse and strange practices of the group. Unfortunately for Jim Jones, the US government still had concerns about the settlement and wanted to keep an eye on their activities. They sent House of Representatives member Leo Ryan to Jonestown to investigate. Before Ryan could return to the United States with his findings, he and several of his companions were murdered by followers of Jones. Soon after, Jones then forced, convinced and coerced over 900 temple members to commit suicide. It is assumed Jones then shot himself – his body was found with a supposed 'self-inflicted gunshot'.

A few years later, in 1980, one of Leo Ryan's top aids came out with a different story. Joe Holsinger was an administrative assistant to Ryan, and he told a newspaper that he had information that suggested a secret branch of the CIA was operating in Guyana at the time of the massacre. He believed that the deaths were caused by a mass mind control experiment – orchestrated by MK-Ultra – and that the government had carefully constructed the idea of the Jonestown cult as a way of covering up their movements.

SOME THEORIES SUGGEST MK-ULTRA CONTINUED IN SECRET AND WAS TO BLAME FOR SOME OF THE MOST HORRIFIC CRIMES OF THE PAST 50 YEARS.

The majority of the 900 temple members drank Flavor Aid laced with cyanide. Those who did not drink it were injected with poison.

AN ENTERTAINING COVER-UP

When *Stranger Things* hit Netflix in 2016, it became an instant hit. The idea of five plucky teens taking on a shady government institution had viewers hooked. But could *Stranger Things*, and other shows in the same vein, actually be part of a larger cover-up?

Marie D Jones co-authored the book *Mind Wars: A History of Mind Control, Surveillance, and Social Engineering by the Government, Media, and Secret Societies*. As part of her research, she looked through pages and pages of declassified material on MK-Ultra. What she discovered was more horrific than she could have imagined. Jones is not a fan of wild conspiracy theories or shows like *Stranger Things*. 'It's important that the truth of MK-Ultra is known,' says Jones. 'But the way it has become so well known in popular culture has also become a bit of a problem.'

Put simply, Jones believes the trivialisation of experiments such as those conducted by MK-Ultra waters down the truth behind the stories, and makes any suggestion that it could still be happening feel like something from the world of science fiction and fantasy. Films and TV shows such as *American Horror Story: Cult*, *The Wicker Man* and *The Master* all play with the idea that cults and mind control are fantastical, entertaining, but not something that could actually happen. Could our enjoyment of these fictional works be the one thing that prevents us from seeing the truth when experiments like MK-Ultra are right under our noses?

HOLLOW EARTH

THE THEORY IN A NUTSHELL

There is a subterranean world 800 miles beneath our feet. It is full of life and may even contain whole civilisations.

MOST OF US LEARNT AT school that the globe is made up of the Earth's surface, a crust made up of rocks and minerals, followed by a liquid magma mantle surrounding a solid iron-nickel alloy core. But what if this was all a lie? What if, 800 miles beneath the surface, the Earth opened into a huge underground world? The theory stretches beyond conspiracy, with many cultures believing in a hidden world. The ancient city of Shambhala, according to some Buddhists, can be located deep inside the Earth, while the ancient Greeks believed a god called Hades ruled the underworld.

A WORLD BENEATH OUR FEET

In 1692, English astronomer and mathematician Edmond Halley (yes, the same Edmond Halley who identified Halley's comet that orbits the Sun roughly every 76 years) suggested that there was another world beneath the surface of the Earth that even had its own atmosphere. He believed that it was this atmosphere that created phenomena seen above the Earth's surface, like the aurora borealis (Northern Lights).

Nearly 100 years later, Le Clerc Milfort took a group of indigenous people called the Muscogee into caves above the Mississippi River in the US. Milfort believed that the Muscogee people originated from a civilisation who once lived under the Earth. In 1818, John Cleves Symmes Jr published a circular (a leaflet or small magazine) that detailed his own ideas. He believed the Earth's core contained a number of solid concentric spheres, that were open at the poles.

RICHARD E. BYRD

In 1926, aviator and adventurer Richard E. Byrd gave support to Symmes' theory that there was an opening to the underworld at the North and South Poles. Conspiracy theorists state that in Byrd's 'secret diary', he claimed to have seen an entrance to an inner world as he flew over the North Pole. It was a place filled with green plants and animals – nothing like the rest of the landscape. Whether Byrd ever reached the North Pole was called into question by Bernt Balchen, an associate of Byrd's. He claimed that Byrd's flight to the North Pole was nothing but an elaborate hoax.

However, the theory persisted, and in 1996, seismologists Xiaodong Song and Paul Richards made the discovery that the Earth's core did not rotate at the same speed as the rest of the Earth. This discovery suggests that there could be open air between the Earth's iron core and the ground beneath our feet.

How the Earth might look if an opening to a secret world was located at the North Pole.

GOING UNDERGROUND

If there is a world below ours, as so many scientists and explorers have suggested over the past 300 years, what could possibly be hidden there? Many religious and fictitious depictions show a world that is lush with trees, grass, plants and animals – much like the scene Richard E. Byrd claimed to have seen from his aircraft in 1926. But how could vegetation grow in a world shielded from the Sun? Simple: theorists believe that there is a sun inside the Earth.

But who, or what, could be living down there? Some theories claim that aliens have made a settlement there, as well as lost Viking tribes. Mythical creatures, such as dragons, and extinct animals might also have found refuge beneath the Earth's surface.

SECRET SOCIETY

Imagine for a moment that there really is a rich, lush world full of plants and minerals just 800 miles beneath our feet. The discovery would be as world-changing as finding life on other planets or proving that time travel is possible. So, it is not beyond the realms of possibility that world leaders would make the collective decision to keep the discovery a secret. The underground world would be the perfect place to escape to and act as a second Earth should the surface of our planet become uninhabitable.

Scientists are openly searching for a 'Planet B', but could they have already found it closer to home? Novelists such as Jules Verne and C.S. Lewis were fascinated by the idea of the Hollow Earth and, similar to the theories discussed, imagined whole civilisations of people and mythical creatures who lived underground. With so much still to learn about the Earth's core and what lies at the centre of our planet, who can really say whether what lay in their imagination might not actually be reality?

IF THERE IS A HOLLOW EARTH BENEATH OUR FEET, WHY IS IT BEING KEPT A SECRET?

CHECK THE SCIENCE

Despite all the theories, the majority of the scientific world still agree that the Earth is not hollow. One of the main reasons can be found when we study seismic waves, created by earthquakes. The way the waves move indicates that the Earth is a solid, layered structure. Gravity and magnetic forces would also be disrupted if the Earth was not layered with soil, minerals, lava and a solid iron core.

HAVANA SYNDROME

THE THEORY IN A NUTSHELL
The Russian government has developed a secret acoustic weapon that can cause severe dizziness, headaches, memory loss and a constant ringing in the ears.

IN 2016, A NUMBER OF PEOPLE working at the US embassy in Havana, Cuba, began to feel unwell. They were all experiencing the same, strange symptoms – vertigo, a foggy head and an unbearable noise ringing in their ears. Despite being checked over by medical staff, doctors could not find any cause for the mystery illness. Immediately, alarm bells began to sound. Could this have been a covert attack on the US embassy by some invisible weapon? The illness was called 'Havana Syndrome' and more cases began to be recorded across the US and beyond.

HOW DOES IT FEEL?

Havana Syndrome was so hard to define at the time of the US embassy event because there had been nothing quite like it before. A loud noise, followed by a cocktail of mind-bending symptoms that only seemed to affect a certain number of people in specific locations. One victim from Florida, US, described a loud noise, followed by a sensation in her ear that was like 'a dentist drilling on steroids'. Investigations concluded that, while it likely wasn't the cause, the symptoms were compounded by pulsed electromagnetic energy from 'external stimuli' that disturbed the function of the brain. With this in mind, theories began to spread as to how and why Havana Syndrome was created.

A COORDINATED ATTACK

With many more cases of Havana Syndrome being recorded around the world, deeper investigations were ordered to find out more about this strange condition. A report on over 300 Americans who presented with Havana Syndrome symptoms showed that nearly all of them were part of the US military, with the majority of sufferers working in the intelligence or defence departments. Further victims around the planet (in countries such as Austria, Poland and China, to name a few) almost always had links to government or official military posts.

Those keen to play down the rumours of Havana Syndrome being used as a weapon in a foreign attack, claimed it could be caused by radio frequencies and ultrasound waves used in the technology associated with military operations.

THE UNCOVERED COVER-UP

Early in 2025, a declassified US Senate report revealed that some of the first reported cases of Havana Syndrome were 'mishandled' by the CIA. Those who reported their health conditions were 'delayed or denied care' they were legally entitled to. The Senate report went on to detail that in the year running up to the CIA's official conclusion that Havana Syndrome was not part of a foreign attack, support for the victims dramatically reduced.

This disinterest might seem baffling to anyone who knows the history of relations between the US and Russia, who are not often shy of reporting suspicious behaviour between the two countries. However, each new US administration has its own agendas, and Trump's warmer relationship with Russia during his second term as president might mean that anything that jeopardises that relationship may be hushed up... for the time being at least.

HAVANA SYNDROME ONLY AFFECTED A CERTAIN SECTION OF SOCIETY.

THE FACE BEHIND THE WAVE

Despite over 1500 cases of Havana Syndrome being reported since 2016, no one has been able to explain what causes it or who is to blame. Some government officials believed the event in 2016 was a coordinated attack by Russia, however an investigation by the CIA claimed there was no evidence to support this. Instead, it suggested various reasons for the symptoms of Havana Syndrome, including neurological and psychological problems with the victims themselves.

Eight years later, in 2024, a joint investigation by media outlets *The Insider* and *Der Spiegel*, and the US TV show *60 Minutes*, claimed to have discovered evidence that linked Havana Syndrome with the shadowy Russian intelligence unit known as 29155. 29155 is tasked with the most secret and dangerous operations in the Russian military and was linked to the attempted death by poisoning of former Russian spy Sergei Skripal in 2018. The investigation claimed that members of the 29155 were stationed in the exact same cities, at the exact same time, when Havana Syndrome was reported. They also discovered that an officer in the 29155 had been given a special award for his work in 'non-lethal acoustic weapons'. After the investigation, representatives from both Russia and the US said that they still did not think there was enough evidence to prove that Havana Syndrome was a Russian weapon. Were the two governments playing down the evidence to keep the peace?

Theories claim Havana Syndrome targeted the human brain, causing headaches and dizziness, amongst other symptoms.

THE DISAPPEARANCE OF AGATHA CHRISTIE

THE THEORY IN A NUTSHELL

The famous crime novelist, Agatha Christie, disappeared for 11 days in 1926, claiming to have lost all memory of who she was – but what really happened to her?

IN 1926, AGATHA CHRISTIE WAS becoming one of the biggest and brightest new literary stars of the UK. She was from a wealthy family, married and had a young daughter called Rosalind. From the outside, Agatha had it all. So, when she disappeared from the family home in Sunningdale in Berkshire, the news hit the headlines. What followed was 11 days of police manhunts, wild speculation, murder accusations and celebrity investigations.

LOST – THEN FOUND

On the evening of 3rd December 1926, Agatha Christie left her family home in Berkshire. The following morning, her car was found above a quarry in Surrey. Its lights were still on, and a fur coat and bag containing Agatha's belongings were found inside – but Agatha herself was nowhere to be seen. The police began looking for some trace of the missing author and a media frenzy began to stir due to the mysterious vanishing. Fellow writer Arthur Conan Doyle – creator of the famous sleuth Sherlock Holmes – even contacted a medium to see if they could discover the whereabouts of Agatha Christie.

Then, 11 days later, a musician who had been playing at the Swan Hydropathic Hotel in Harrogate, UK, reported seeing Agatha as one of the guests. Sure enough, the writer was staying at the hotel, and had been there all along. She claimed she had no memory of who she was, or how she had got there. Archie Christie, Agatha's husband, made his way to the hotel. He told the waiting crowd of newspaper reporters that his wife had suffered a nervous breakdown – but his excuse wasn't good enough for the press. After 11 days of mystery, surely there was something more to the story?

THE TRUTH BEHIND THE HEADLINES

During the search, and for many weeks after Agatha Christie had been found, wild stories circulated in the top newspapers in the UK. Some questioned Agatha's husband and suggested that he might have murdered Agatha and hidden her body – a theory straight from one of Agatha's novels. Others believed that the disappearance was a publicity stunt, constructed to sell more of Agatha's books or even to tease the storyline of her next novel.

Another theory grew from the name that Agatha used to check into the Swan Hydropathic Hotel – Teresa Neele. Neele was the surname of the woman Archie Christie was not only having an affair with, but the woman he wanted to leave Agatha for. Could Agatha have been so angry with her husband that she wanted to publicly humiliate him with her disappearance or even have him framed for her murder? Despite the scandal and accusations, the Christies held firm with their story: Agatha had suffered from some form of mental illness.

The Swan Hydropathic Hotel in Harrogate, where Agatha Christie was found staying during her disappearance.

A FUGUE STATE

Even years after her 11-day disappearance, Agatha Christie always maintained that she had suffered a nervous breakdown. It was rumoured that after she returned to her everyday life, she began to see a doctor in Harley Street for treatment, although no medical records have ever proven that Agatha was seen by a psychiatrist. But perhaps there are clues of her experience in her writing? She wrote a book called *Giant's Bread* – published in 1930 – which told the story of a composer who lost his memory. Tellingly, she wrote the novel under her pseudonym, Mary Westmacott.

After Agatha and Archie finally divorced a couple of years later, Agatha told the story of her disappearance to the *Daily Mail* – the best-selling newspaper in the UK at the time. In it, she described what we now know to be a fugue state, where the mind disassociates from a painful reality. On the night of her disappearance, Archie had told Agatha he was leaving her and had gone to spend the weekend with Nancy Neele. Agatha could not cope with what was happening to her, so her mind created a safe reality for her to temporarily exist in.

> AGATHA CHRISTIE CHECKED INTO THE HOTEL UNDER THE NAME TERESA NEELE.

FROM DARKNESS COMES LIGHT

Following her disappearance (and her divorce from Archie Christie) Agatha went on to write 60 more novels, and arguably some of her best and most famous works. She also found time to see the world. She booked a passage on the Orient Express and travelled to Egypt – inspiring two of her best-loved novels. Her books began to be made into films, and she became one of the UK's most beloved writers. Whatever the truth behind her disappearance – publicity stunt, mental breakdown or hoax – Agatha became stronger because of it.

THE SINKING OF THE TITANIC

THE THEORY IN A NUTSHELL

The sinking of RMS *Titanic* was not a tragic accident caused by a stray iceberg...

TITANIC WAS THE 'UNSINKABLE' ship. This doomed phrase still haunts the tragedy over 100 years later, but why did so many people think this way? *Titanic*'s 'unsinkable' tag grew in popularity when details of the ship's state-of-the-art design were revealed, along with its revolutionary, never-before-seen safety features. Marketing agencies loved the moniker and used it to sell passages on *Titanic*. With so much confidence in the 'unsinkable' ship – a liner more advanced than any that had gone before – could something else have caused *Titanic* to flounder?

DEADLY BUSINESS RIVALS

J. P. Morgan was rich, powerful and used to getting what he wanted. He also happened to be one of the owners of the White Star Line who operated *Titanic* and her sister ships. At the time *Titanic* set sail, Morgan was battling to create the Federal Reserve – the central banking system in the US – but not all his business buddies were onboard with his plan.

It just so happened that some of Morgan's biggest rivals – Jacob Astor, Isidor Straus and Benjamin Guggenheim – were on board the *Titanic* when it sank. One theory suggests that Morgan used his contacts to ensure that all three men never saw another day of trading again. One detail that has made this theory stand the test of time is that Morgan himself was also due to set sail on the *Titanic*'s maiden voyage, but suspiciously changed his mind at the last minute. Was this a lucky escape, or did Morgan know something his rivals did not?

SECRET SWITCH

One thing we all know about the *Titanic* is that its wreckage lies beneath the Atlantic Ocean, just off the coast of Canada. Or does it? One theory believes that this is actually the remains of *Titanic*'s sister ship, RMS *Olympic*. *Olympic* was in service for a year before *Titanic* set sail, and had already been in a serious collision with a navy warship called HMS *Hawke*. The battered ship was then sent to the same shipyard where, coincidentally, *Titanic* was being built.

The repairs to *Olympic* were so expensive that White Star Line made the decision to simply switch the names on the near-identical ships. *Olympic* was patched up and sent off to sea as *Titanic*, laden with explosives that would detonate and sink the ship. The huge insurance payout White Star Line received was a far better outcome than having to spend thousands on *Olympic*'s repairs. And as for the 'real' *Titanic*? It carried on as a passenger liner and retired in 1935.

As well as their size, the fact the *Titanic* and *Olympic were* described as 'unsinkable' was a huge draw for potential customers.

AN EGYPTIAN CURSE

One of the spookier theories on what truly caused *Titanic* to sink revolves around the story of the Unlucky Mummy. The wooden casket, adorned with wide, staring eyes, was believed to once contain the body of an Egyptian princess. It is believed to cause catastrophe wherever it goes as revenge for being taken from its home country. Currently housed in the British Museum, it has also been blamed for the disappearance of two women and numerous mishaps inside the museum itself. The Unlucky Mummy was believed to have been in *Titanic*'s haul, on its way to New York to be displayed, when disaster struck. The item was never documented on any of *Titanic*'s paperwork, and despite claims that it never even left the British Museum, this theory is still one of the most popular today.

IMAGES OF THE TITANIC IN A SCRAPYARD BEGAN CIRCULATING ONLINE IN 2023.

POWERS OF NATURE

You only have to look at the hundreds of books, documentaries and films that have been created on the subject of *Titanic* to see that it remains fascinating to both historians and amateur sleuths alike. Despite the theories that continue to swirl around the ship, the most-likely conclusion remains: on the morning of 14th April 1912, the *Titanic* hit an iceberg – estimated to be around 120 m long – floating much further south than icebergs are usually found at that time of year.

The damage caused was catastrophic and prompted an overhaul in the safety of nautical navigation. What *Titanic* proved was that even an 'unsinkable' ship was not immune to the powers of nature.

GEOENGINEERING

THE THEORY IN A NUTSHELL

The practice devised to help combat global warming is actually a cover-up to create extreme weather and spread population-controlling chemicals.

GEOENGINEERING ISN'T A conspiracy theory in itself. In fact, it is a government-approved, worldwide technique being proposed to help combat climate issues, and covers carbon dioxide removal and solar radiation management. Put simply, geoengineering sucks carbon dioxide out of the atmosphere and reflects sunlight back out into space and both practices aim to help cool down the Earth and slow down global warming. No problems there, right? Unless, of course, geoengineering is taken a step further, and used to control populations and create natural disasters, as some people believe...

TRACING LINES

Have you ever looked up at the sky on a bright, clear day and traced the trail of an aeroplane, wondering which exotic location it might be jetting off to? Those trails are commonly known as contrails and are formed when water vapour and soot particulates from burning jet fuel freeze into ice crystals. As well as being one of the major environmental concerns of our time, these trails have also sparked a theory within the geoengineering sphere. It has been suggested that those criss-crossing white lines are not simply the emissions from the aircraft, but chemtrails.

In the 1990s, researchers Richard Finke and William Thomas posted their concerns over chemtrails on internet forums and declared that the United States Air Force was spreading 'mysterious substances' onto the population below. The chemtrails have been blamed for creating extreme weather, population control and even mind control.

UP, UP AND AWAY

With around 100,000 aeroplanes taking off across the world each day, chemtrails would certainly be a quick, large-scale and effective way to change the world for anyone who wanted to. But what purpose would this serve? One school of thought believes that chemtrails are being used to control overpopulation. The chemicals being pumped into the air by numerous commercial and domestic flights could contain substances that affect fertility – meaning less children are born – as well as causing diseases that attack the most vulnerable in society. Mind control airborne drugs could be used to change a country's perception and beliefs, while a natural disaster could have benefits for insurance scams and certain businesses.

Despite all this conjecture, there is no hard evidence to suggest that chemtrails really do exist. The World Health Organization, NASA, meteorologists and The British Airline Pilots' Association have all stated that there is no evidential basis for the theory.

THE WEATHER IS BEING MANIPULATED BY THE MILITARY.

HIDING IN PLAIN SIGHT

Created in 1993, HAARP (High-Frequency Active Auroral Research Program) studies the ionosphere – the ionized part of the Earth's atmosphere that extends into space. Officially, HAARP's main area of interest is focused on radio waves, and how these interact with navigational systems around the world. However, it has also been the focus of some very concerning theories. It has been suggested that HAARP, under the guidance of the US Air Force, has been able to use its technology and findings to affect the weather and bring about natural disasters, as well as turning it into a form of weaponry. Its studies into radio frequencies have also led to HAARP being accused of interfering with military communications.

PLAYING GOD

If geoengineering can control sunlight enough to bounce it back into space, surely it could be used to direct sunlight wherever it needs to go? With this in mind, some theorists suggest that companies who rely on the Sun at certain times for production will be able to use it however they please for the biggest profit. More concerning, this technique can also be used to create devastating droughts, creating a natural disaster and upheaval for millions. When technology is created, it can often be used for good and bad – could geoengineering have been sabotaged to make money by playing God with sunlight?

An example of a 'space mirror' satellite that could be used to help control the amount of sunlight that reaches the Earth.

AN ALL-TOO-EASY SOLUTION

While geoengineering continues to be researched and experiments conducted to help the environment, there are some climate activists who are worried about the practice for a number of reasons. Their main concern is that geoengineering will be seen as some kind of 'solution' to climate change by unwilling governments and big industries. If these institutions see geoengineering as a way to stop the Earth heating up, they could abandon all the legislations and promises put into place over the past two decades to help stop global warming. Why spend time and money doing something in an eco-friendly way, when we can simply suck out the carbon and bounce sunlight back out of the Earth's atmosphere? Activists suggest that geoengineering is a plaster to a much bigger, wide-scale problem.

THE LAST FLIGHT OF AMELIA EARHART

THE THEORY IN A NUTSHELL

When the ground-breaking pilot, Amelia Earhart, went missing in 1937, the public was not told the whole story.

AMELIA EARHART WAS BORN in 1897 in Kansas, US. She loved adventure and, after visiting an air show in Toronto with a friend, she fell in love with flying. In 1921 she began flying lessons and in 1932 she became the first woman to fly solo across the Atlantic. Amelia was also the first person, male or female, to fly from Hawaii to Oakland, California. But her flying adventures were about to take a tragic turn.

A pair of aviation goggles similar to those worn by Amelia Earhart.

GLOBE-TROTTING DISASTER

In 1937, aged 40, Amelia wanted to fly around the globe. She enlisted the help of navigator Fred Noonan and set off from Oakland, California on the 1st June. Despite only having 7000 miles left of their epic 29,000-mile journey, Amelia and Fred's plane was lost between Lae and Howland Island in the Pacific Ocean. A huge search was conducted, but all traces of Amelia, Fred and their plane were lost. Despite numerous investigations and possible sightings of the plane wreckage (some as recent as 2024), questions still remain unanswered as to why Amelia Earhart did not complete her journey.

A SIGN OF THE TIMES

The search for Amelia Earhart was the most expensive rescue operation ever seen in the United States. When nothing was found, a report was drawn up to satisfy the waiting public, who had followed every moment of the story in the newspapers. The report concluded that Amelia's plane had run out of fuel and crashed into the ocean, and Amelia and Fred were declared dead in 1939. In the immediate aftermath of the event, Amelia and Fred were blamed for whatever mistakes led to the disaster. Amelia was considered by a minority to have made an error to take on such a challenge, and Fred was even exposed as an alcoholic. Later, colleagues of Fred Noonan confirmed that Fred often turned up to jobs looking 'hungover' but that he was still one of the best navigators in the world.

As for the criticism of Amelia, we only have to look at the way women were viewed in the 1930s. Women had not long won the right to vote, and were certainly not seen as equals of men when it came to aviation and adventuring. It would have been easy for the (mostly male) journalists, pilots and government officials to paint a picture of Amelia as incompetent – rather than pushing themselves to discover the truth.

AMELIA THE SPY

In 2017, a black and white photograph, believed to have been taken in the late-1930s on the then-Japanese Marshall Islands, was discovered in the US National Archives. The picture, possibly taken by a US spy, shows a figure that bears a striking resemblance to Amelia Earhart. Although the figure has their back to the camera, the posture and hairstyle are very similar to Amelia's. What's more, another figure in the picture seems to resemble her navigator, Fred Noonan.

So, if this image really does show Amelia and Fred to be alive and well, what does it mean? For years, Amelia was rumoured to have been a spy – using her aviation skills to fly over suspected enemy territories and deliver information back to President Roosevelt. One theory suggests that Amelia's trip around the globe was merely a cover-up for a spy mission to Japan. When Amelia went missing, the US government did not want it to be known that she and Fred had been taken prisoner by the Japanese. Instead, they constructed the idea that Amelia's plane had run out of fuel and crashed. However, could this photo prove that she had been discovered as a spy and been captured instead?

AN ISLAND CRASH-LANDING

Amelia Earhart had already travelled 22,000 miles when she landed in Lae, New Guinea. The next, and final, part of her trip was to cross the huge Pacific Ocean, stopping briefly on the tiny Howland Island to refuel, before returning to Oakland, California. However, Amelia Earhart and Fred Noonan never made it to Howland Island. During the search, pilots flew over the uninhabited island of Nikumaroro, then called Gardner Island. The island is 400 miles southeast of Howland Island and showed 'signs of recent habitation'. As they mistakenly believed the island was already inhabited, this lead wasn't considered strong enough to follow up on. On one of the reconnaissance trips, human bones, a woman's shoe, a tool identical to one used by Fred Noonan and a bottle of herbal liqueur was found. The bones were studied but dismissed as having anything to do with the disaster.

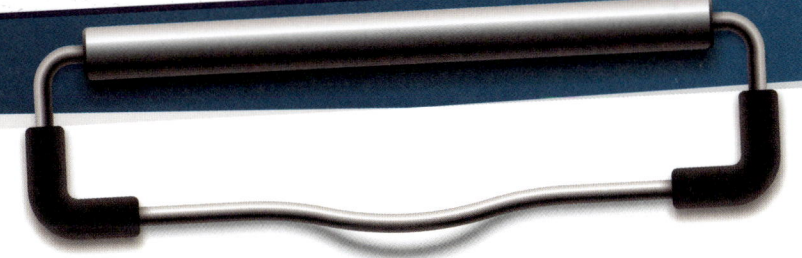

A photo was discovered, possibly showing Amelia Earhart alive and well.

SEARCHING FOR THE TRUTH

From the late-1980s through to the 2000s, The International Group for Historic Aircraft Recovery made many trips to Nikumaroro in an attempt to discover what happened. They claimed to have discovered traces of campfires, beauty products from the 1930s, clamshells that looked as though they had been opened with tools, and even more human bones. Although the bones disappeared, their findings were re-examined in 2018 using new technology. The research concluded that 'Earhart is more similar to the Nikumaroro bones than 99 per cent of individuals in a large reference sample'. Could this be the proof the world has been waiting for?

THE BEAST OF GÉVAUDAN

THE THEORY IN A NUTSHELL

A series of wolf attacks that killed multiple people in eighteenth-century France was, in fact, a strange unidentified beast that has been covered up for generations.

NOT ALL CONSPIRACY THEORIES have been dreamt up in the last 100 years. In fact, some go as far back as 1764, to the quiet farming region of Gévaudan in France (now known as the département of Lozère). Over the course of a few years, over 50 people were attacked and eaten by a wild wolf – at least, that is what was first thought to have been to blame. More than 250 years later, historians are still analysing witness statements from the time, trying to discover what the 'beast' could truly have been.

UNPRECEDENTED ATTACKS

On 30th June 1764, Jeanne Boulet was tending her flock of sheep in Gévaudan when she was savagely attacked and killed by a wild beast. Just two months before, another young woman was looking after a herd of cattle when she, too, was attacked. Luckily for her, and for those studying the story, she survived to give an account of what she endured. In her own words she described the creature as being 'like a wolf, yet not a wolf'. For agricultural workers at that time, wolves would have been an occupational hazard, something they were used to spotting and keeping their sheep and cattle protected from, so for such a creature to have attacked and killed, it would have had to have been something out of the norm. Over the following months, more attacks were reported and the news travelled across Europe and beyond. Men, women and children fell victim to the beast – with some people arguing that there were, in fact, more than one of them. When an attack was reported in late 1765, a group of men tried to flush out the beast. Despite opening fire on a shadowy creature, it escaped.

CHILD HEROES AND A ROYAL DECREE

Earlier in 1765, the beast targeted a group of children aged between 10–12. This brave bunch of kids fought back and managed to scare the creature off. The story became so infamous, that King Louis XV heard about it and decided to reward them, even funding one of the children's education.

Now the news of the Gévaudan Beast had reached the royal palace, King Louis was determined to do something about it. He offered up a vast sum of money to anyone who could capture the beast. Any large wolf was now a target. In fact, in late-1765, the beast was supposedly captured by one of the King's own gunmen.

A ROYAL COVER-UP

The body of the supposed beast that was responsible for so many deaths was sent to King Louis and the reward was duly given. But not all was as it seemed. Despite being large, and somewhat ferocious, the creature was most definitely a wolf – something that went against many of its previous descriptions. Sure enough, a few months later, the attacks began again. King Louis, however, did not want to look as though he had given the reward to the wrong person. He ignored the reports and insisted that the beast had been caught.

In 1767, two years after the first attack, a nobleman called Marquis d'Apcher took matters into his own hands and organised a search for the beast. A creature was captured by one of the party, local farmer Jean Chastel. When the body was examined, they discovered human remains inside, and non-wolf-like features. Finally, the attacks stopped, but the mystery over what the creature was remained.

PREHISTORIC CREATURE OR... SERIAL KILLER?

Like all good mysteries, there have been many theories as to what the creature was. Some theories suggest it was simply a large wolf, a hyena or even a strange hybrid of dog and wolf. Descriptions of the creature at the time note that it was as big as a lion or a small horse, with a strong tail and talon-like claws. Although it seems unlikely, one theory suggests a similarity between the description of the beast and the extinct *Hyaenodon* that last roamed the earth over 25 million years ago. Just as followers of the Loch Ness monster believe that somehow a plesiosaur had survived extinction in a Scottish loch, some theorists claim that this species of hyaenodon was alive and well in France in the 1700s.

Finally, and most chillingly, some believe that there was no beast at all. Rather, they think that it was a crazed serial killer dressed as an animal to avoid detection. The only proof for this theory is that many of the victims were decapitated, which is something wolves do not tend to do. However, could decapitation have been a feature of the *Hyaenodon*, or some other mythical, wolf-like creature?

A monument to Jean Chastel can be seen at La Besseyre-Saint-Mary, France.

THE BEAST WAS DESCRIBED AS BEING LIKE A WOLF, YET NOT A WOLF.

THE VAMPIRE OF NEW ENGLAND

THE THEORY IN A NUTSHELL

In the late 1800s a vampire plagued the Brown family of Exeter, New England, in the United States.

IN 1892, THE FARMING community of Exeter, New England, was suffering from a strange wasting disease – with one family in particular suffering more than most. Was it a wave of tuberculosis (called 'consumption' at the time) or something far more sinister?

FAMILY LOSS

The Brown family was a normal, God-fearing farming family. They were well-liked in Exeter and everyone was saddened to hear of the death of Mary Elizabeth Arnold Brown, the wife of George and mother to seven children. The news was shocking to anyone who knew Mary, as she was a strong woman who helped her husband on the farm. To add to their grief, Mary Olive Brown, the eldest daughter, passed away six months later. The cause of death for both mother and daughter was recorded as consumption.

The Brown family continued with their lives until Edwin, the only son in the family, started to show signs of the illness. He decided to move away from Exeter with his wife to regain his strength, and the plan seemed to be working until he was forced to return home. Two years after his mother and sister had passed away, Edwin's sister Mercy died of a short, quick battle with consumption. Edwin came back to Exeter to be with his father, but it was to be the deadliest decision he ever made.

BLOOD CONNECTION

Now he was back in Exeter, Edwin's old illness began to return. His once healthy complexion turned sallow and his muscles wasted away. People around him commented that it seemed as though his life and blood were being drained away. Some sources claim Edwin had been ill before his return to Exeter, but by this time, the concept of vampires was popular in the US thanks to Gothic novels. Maybe this contributed to people's imaginations getting the better of them? Indeed, the dramatic change in Edwin's health led one group of men in Exeter to the assumption that one of the deceased Brown family women was, in fact, leaving their grave at night to suck the life out of Edwin. In his fear for Edwin's health, George agreed to let the men exhume the graves of his wife and two daughters.

What they found would send shockwaves across the country, and inspire countless stories and legends. George's wife, Mary, and his eldest daughter were exhumed and looked as they would expect to look after being buried for many years. Mercy, who had been buried around two months before her exhumation, looked very different. It is said that the men 'stepped back in terror' when they saw her body.

Mercy looked as though she could have been sleeping. She was fresh-faced and, chillingly, 'filled with fresh blood'. The men instantly believed that Mercy was a vampire, living off her brother Edwin. Her heart was removed and burned, and, gruesomely, the ashes were given to Edwin as medicine. However, the medicine did not work and Edwin died two months later.

Mercy Brown, the woman thought to have been a vampire.

FAMILY CURSE

With Edwin gone, George hoped it would be the end of his family's tragic story. However, there was more to come. Of George's remaining four daughters, only one survived to live a long and healthy life. Annie, Jennie and Myra each died as young adults, shortly after they were married – each of the same wasting illness that had taken their mother and siblings. Many in Exeter believed that Mercy was preying on her siblings and taking each one with her to the underworld. When Edwin was in his last days, delirious with fever, he repeated: 'She was here, she wants me to come with her!'

When such tragedies keep occurring within the same family, it's tempting to look towards the supernatural and the monstrous to try and justify how such terrible luck could befall a single family. However, in the late-1800s, tuberculosis was rife and had a high mortality rate. The germs spread through the air when someone suffering from the disease coughed, sneezed or simply spoke, making it even more likely that those close to them would likely catch it themselves.

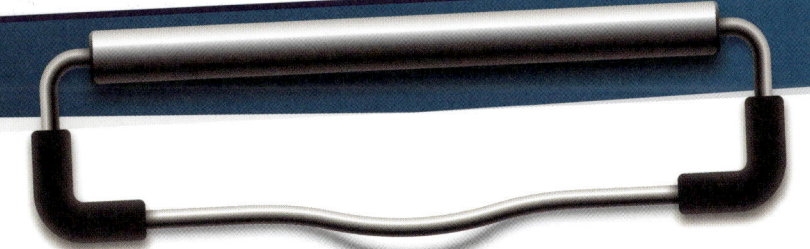

WHEN EXHUMED, MERCY'S BODY LOOKED AS IF SHE WAS SIMPLY SLEEPING.

A LEGEND IN THE MAKING

When *Dracula* author Bram Stoker died, the story of Mercy and the Brown family was found among his papers. Historians have theorised that the character of Lucy in *Dracula* was based on Mercy. The story went on to inspire other works such as Sarah L. Thomson's young adult novel *Mercy: The Last New England Vampire* and H.P. Lovecraft's *The Shunned House*. Mercy's grave remains at the Chestnut Hill Cemetery in Exeter and is visited by vampire enthusiasts and literary fans to this day.

ANIMAL SPIES

THE THEORY IN A NUTSHELL

The CIA used cats, insects and pigeons to spy on their enemies. Most official reports say that the project was short-lived, but could that all be part of the plan?

IN 2001, PREVIOUSLY confidential files were released to the public containing details of a plan called 'Acoustic Kitty'. The plan, which was conceived in the 1960s, aimed to use cats as a way of spying on foreign embassies. It might sound like something dreamt up by the overactive imagination of a screenwriter, but Acoustic Kitty actually did happen. In one report, a cat was said to have had a microphone inserted into its ear, a radio transmitter placed at the base of its skull and an antenna woven into its fur. As well as being incredibly cruel by today's standards, the plan was not as successful as the CIA had hoped.

MISSION IMPOSSIBLE

Acoustic Kitty's first mission was to head to a public park, close to the Russian Embassy, and listen in to a conversation between two men on a bench. The aim was to obtain intelligence on what was being discussed outside of the embassy's walls – a place where the two men thought they were safe from prying ears.

With everything set up, Acoustic Kitty was released. Unfortunately, the official reports say that the cat got distracted and ended up running into traffic. However, that might not be the whole story.

MISSION... POSSIBLE?

In their book, *Spycraft*, H. Keith Melton and Robert Wallace discuss the multiple types of animal they trained to 'spy' on targets. In it, they describe the use of a cat as part of a surveillance operation on an Asian head of state. The cat could wander in and out of meeting rooms without attracting any attention. The cat picked up some useful information, but the team wanted more. In fact, they wanted to be able to control where the cat went. Working with Robin Michelson, who was one of the inventors of the human cochlear implant, they implanted a wire into the cat that could be used to control its movements with ultrasonic sound waves. There are differing accounts as to what happened to the cat. Some say it ran into traffic, but others claimed it went on to live a long life. So what should we believe? There are three possibilities:

1. The cat had been so badly tampered with that it died because of the cruel procedures it was put through – not a good look for the CIA. So, the story of the cat running away was rolled out to cover their tracks.

2. Acoustic Kitty was so successful the CIA wanted to keep their new undercover animal spy a secret. They reported that the cat had died so that no one would look at a passing kitty with suspicion.

3. The cat did run off the first chance it had – and who could blame it?

BIRDS AREN'T REAL!

In 2017, Peter McIndoe was visiting a friend in Memphis, Tennessee when he started the Birds Aren't Real movement. The movement suggested that, some time ago, all the birds in the world died out and were replaced by robots, used as surveillance on the population. The movement grew and grew, with bumper stickers and websites catching on to the theory. Could the technology developed in the 1960s have evolved into something far bigger? In a word, no. McIndoe was actually trying to prove a point about how quickly misinformation can be spread across the internet. He joined a protest in Memphis and wrote the silliest thing he could think of on a piece of cardboard. When people asked him what 'birds don't exist' meant, he came up with this wild theory – which a lot of people believed.

ANIMAL KINGDOM

Although the Birds Aren't Real movement is most definitely a hoax, set up to prove an important point, animals being used for surveillance and warfare is all too real, with documents proving that dogs and even insects have been trained and modified to assist humans. Carrier pigeons were used in the Second World War to carry top secret messages, while dogs were used as lookouts and scouts. On Park Lane in London, there is a monument to animals who have served and died in war.

So, as more documents are released detailing past experiments with animals, perhaps we will one day see more feline spies – though hopefully trained with more humane methods.

ARE BIRDS REAL, OR ARE THEY ROBOTS SENT TO SPY ON US?

What began as a joke by a single person grew into a full-blown movement.

THE BUSINESS COUP PLOT

THE THEORY IN A NUTSHELL

In 1933, the newly elected President of the United States, Franklin D. Roosevelt (FDR), was nearly overthrown – and a fascist dictator put in his place.

WHEN ROOSEVELT WAS ELECTED in 1933, the US was in a bad way. The stock market crash had put millions out of work, and people could no longer afford the mortgages or rent for their homes. Roosevelt wanted to abolish poverty – and one of the ways he wanted to do that was to target the rich and redistribute wealth. Despite winning the election, not everyone in the US was happy with FDR's plan. In a world that was growing more and more right-wing (Hitler and Mussolini's popularity was growing by the day) could the rich and powerful men of America team together to take down Roosevelt, protect their wealth and stop him from putting his plan into action?

AMERICA FIRST

You may think that 'America First' is a relatively new phrase, coined by Donald Trump during his presidential campaigns, however, the motto can be traced back to 1916, prior to the United States entering the First World War. President Woodrow Wilson used 'America First' to describe the United States as a world leader, but publishing magnate William Randolph Hearst took the phrase and twisted it.

Hearst did not want Roosevelt as president and was incensed when he won. He emblazoned his newspapers with 'America First' and published articles by Adolf Hitler. In Hearst's eyes, Hitler was doing great things for Germany and Hearst wanted a leader who would do the same. Roosevelt's left-wing, wealth-baiting policies would have been galling for Hearst. It was time to come up with a new motto – and a new way of running the United States.

AMERICAN LIBERTY LEAGUE

While Hearst was using his newspapers to spread his message, a group of wealthy business owners were coming together, pooling their power and resources. The American Liberty League was believed to have included the banker J.P. Morgan, Robert Sterling Clark – the heir to the Singer sewing machine company – and the chief executives of General Motors and Birds Eye.

These powerful men had come together in response to Roosevelt's victory and aimed to teach the government 'the necessity of respect for the rights of persons and property'. They believed that a fascist government, such as the Nazi party in Germany, was the right approach for the US. All they needed was the right person to lead. A respectable man who would automatically have the admiration of thousands of ordinary American people. Who better, then, than a First World War hero?

MAJOR GENERAL BUTLER

Major General Smedley Darlington Butler, to give him his full title, was a highly decorated and respected United States Marine Corps Officer who had fought in multiple wars. He had the support of thousands of veterans as well as serving military – all in all, the perfect choice to lead a coup on the American government. Butler claimed that he had been approached by a man called Gerald P. MacGuire to lead a march on Washington, backed by 500,000 ex-soldiers. The American Liberty League had put millions of dollars behind the plan, and wanted to oust Roosevelt and his government – replacing it with a fascist regime. Butler went on record to tell the world what he had been asked to do, but coming clean did not do Butler many favours.

All of the men believed to have been involved denied any plan to overthrow the government – and many laughed off the suggestion. The man who had first approached Butler was dismissed as a 'prankster' and Butler was made to look as though he had been the victim of a cruel joke. However, we only know so much about Butler's statement due to the fact that he had been subpoenaed by the congressional committee to reveal what he knew. His words were filmed and his testimony was heard far and wide. If the coup had all been a practical joke, it was a joke that was being taken very seriously by all concerned.

THE PHRASE AMERICA FIRST WAS TAKEN BY WILLIAM RANDOLPH HEARST AND TWISTED TO SUIT HIS OWN NARRATIVE.

Butler's testimony was filmed and seen by people throughout the United States.

THE WRONG GUY?

In later years, Major General Smedley Darlington Butler wrote a book and gave talks against war profiteering. He became a spokesperson for the American League Against War and Fascism, donated much of his earnings to the Philadelphia unemployment relief and campaigned for veterans of the First World War to receive financial aid. Knowing this, we can come to two logical conclusions. Firstly, that the American Liberty League saw how popular Butler was and wanted to use his thousands of followers to further, and add credibility to, their cause. Alternatively, could Butler have made the plot up as a way of exposing the big businesses he said were profiting from war?

THE PENDLE SWINDLE

THE THEORY IN A NUTSHELL

In 1633, 17 witches were discovered in the town of Pendle, UK – all thanks to the testimony of a young boy named Edmund Robinson Jr.

BEING A WOMAN IN THE seventeenth century was not easy. Especially when the word of a 10-year-old boy was taken more seriously than your own. In 1612, the small town of Pendle in Lancashire, UK, had already been the scene of an infamous witch trial. But when, in 1633, Edmund Robinson Jr told his tale, another round of accusations began.

SEASON OF THE WITCH

When we hit the end of October, it's hard to go into a shop, stroll along a residential street or scroll on social media without seeing a witch. The ones with the pointy black hats and long noses, clutching to a broomstick. They are characters from storybooks and a popular choice for a Halloween costume.

However, jump back 400 years and the word 'witch' becomes something altogether more frightening. Firstly, because a large section of society believed that witches were real, and that dark magic could cause anything from crop failures to the spreading of disease.

Secondly, if you were a woman in certain circumstances, you could be accused of being a witch. If your husband had died, if you sang to yourself or even fell out with your neighbour, a woman could be accused of witchcraft and trialled.

INFERNAL DEVICES

Just over 20 years before Edmund Robinson made his accusations, Pendle had been the site of an infamous witch trial. A dozen people had been accused of casting curses and harming people with potions and charms. Alizon Device, her brother James and their mother Elizabeth were all among the accused who were put on trial in Lancaster Castle. Their accuser? Alizon's 9-year-old sister, Jennet Device!

Of the 12 people accused, 10 were convicted and hanged, though it is unclear if Alizon was among them. Many people in Pendle would have remembered the Device family, and the other people convicted of witchcraft. It would not have taken much for the town to be convinced that it was happening again.

A TALL TALE

Edmund's story began when he came home one November day, dirty and dishevelled. He told his parents that he had been playing with two greyhounds when they turned into women and kidnapped him. Edmund claimed he was taken to a barn filled with witches, who were eating the most magnificent food. The story soon spread, with news that witches were 'back' in Pendle. Edmund's father began to charge people a small fee to listen to his son's story, as well as taking him to churches to point out any of the witches that he had seen who might be in the congregation. He also resorted to even more unsavoury methods of sourcing money, such as blackmailing villagers so their names would be spared from his son's wagging tongue.

Soon the authorities began to take an interest. Edmund gave the names of many local people who he claimed were at the sabbath – a meeting of witches. Strangely enough, a record shows that one of the names on his list was Jennet Device. Could this be the same Jennet who had testified against her sister 20 years earlier, or simply a coincidence? The woman was the same age as Jennet would have been at that time – and if she still lived in Pendle she would have been an easy target for Edmund's accusations.

> EDMUND'S FATHER WOULD BLACKMAIL PEOPLE, STATING THAT IF THEY DIDN'T PAY, HIS SON WOULD ACCUSE THEM OF BEING A WITCH.

James I brought in the 1604 Act Against Witchcraft, making witchcraft an act punishable by death.

ON TRIAL

Edmund, accompanied by his father, finally accused 17 people of witchcraft. The trial date was set and the gallows built. If they were found guilty, the 17 'witches' would have been hanged, and it would have been one of the biggest witch trials ever to have been recorded. Luckily, George Long, the Justice of the Peace at the time, made the decision to speak to Edmund once more, and this is where Edmund admitted the truth. He had made up the whole story to avoid getting in trouble for coming home with messy clothes and hair. We can also assume that he maintained his story further once his father discovered he could make a bit of money by charging people to hear it.

The 17 people accused were acquitted – however, records show that Jennet Device was still in prison three years later in 1636. Historians believe this is because of a system where, innocent or not, prisoners had to pay for their time in jail. If they could not pay, they had to stay in jail. Despite Edmund's story being revealed as a lie, innocent people were still left to pick up the pieces after being falsely accused.

CELEBRITY BODY DOUBLES

THE THEORY IN A NUTSHELL

When celebrities need to attend an event or be spotted in public but are otherwise unavailable, they employ the use of a lookalike to fill in.

GOSSIP WEBSITES, NEWSPAPERS and social media outlets love a good celebrity spot – especially when they turn up somewhere unexpected. What happens, however, when a celebrity needs to be seen out and about, but they can't be there in person? They might be ill, have fallen out with whoever they need to be spotted with or perhaps there is something more sinister going on behind the scenes…

A ROYAL MIX-UP

When the Princess of Wales took a step back from royal duties following health issues in 2024, the media, and indeed the British public, were sent into a whirlwind of speculation. Princess Kate had not been seen for many weeks when footage of her and the Prince of Wales at a farm shop emerged. It was certainly on brand for the royal couple, who try to enjoy as normal a life as possible, except for one thing: some people were suggesting the woman in the photo did not look quite right. Although she had the same long, dark hair as the princess, her facial features looked out of place.

A few weeks earlier, Kate had been involved in another photographic scandal when an image of her and her three children, released on Mother's Day, was shown to be badly edited in Photoshop. As we now know, the princess had been undergoing cancer treatment, but at the time the royal family had wanted to keep this news under wraps. Could the staged trip to the farm shop with a body double, and the débâcle with the edited photo, all be part of the couple's efforts to keep the princess's health issues a secret for as long as possible? If so, the behaviour of the media made this plan, however well-intentioned, next to impossible to pull off.

MISSING IN MUSIC

The iconic cover of *Abbey Road* by The Beatles has become an internationally recognised image. Thousands of people visit the humble zebra crossing in St John's Wood, London, each year to recreate the shot of the four members crossing the road in perfect unison. However, look a little closer and you will notice that one band member, Sir Paul McCartney, is barefoot. This simple choice was made supposedly because his shoes were too tight. But as some cultures bury their dead without their shoes, this led some fans to believe that Paul McCartney died in 1966 and was replaced by a lookalike. Theorists claim that the rest of the band's outfits confirm their suspicions: John Lennon all in white has been theorised as him representing a religious leader or embodying the colour of mourning expressed in some Eastern religions; Ringo all in black as the funeral director or simply wearing traditional funeral wear; and George Harrison all in denim as a gravedigger.

COMPLICATED

Another musical mystery occurred a little more recently and revolved around Canadian singer and guitarist Avril Lavigne. In 2011, a Brazilian website claimed that Avril had passed away. Rumours persisted that Avril had died by suicide following the death of her grandfather, and that she had been replaced by a woman named Melissa. Melissa had been used by Avril as a doppelgänger so she could avoid gangs of press and escape unseen from parties and events, so, when Avril died, music executives asked Melissa to take her place. Of course, both singing superstars deny and laugh off any suggestion that they are not who they really claim to be! But, as with all good conspiracy theories, that's exactly what we'd expect, right...?

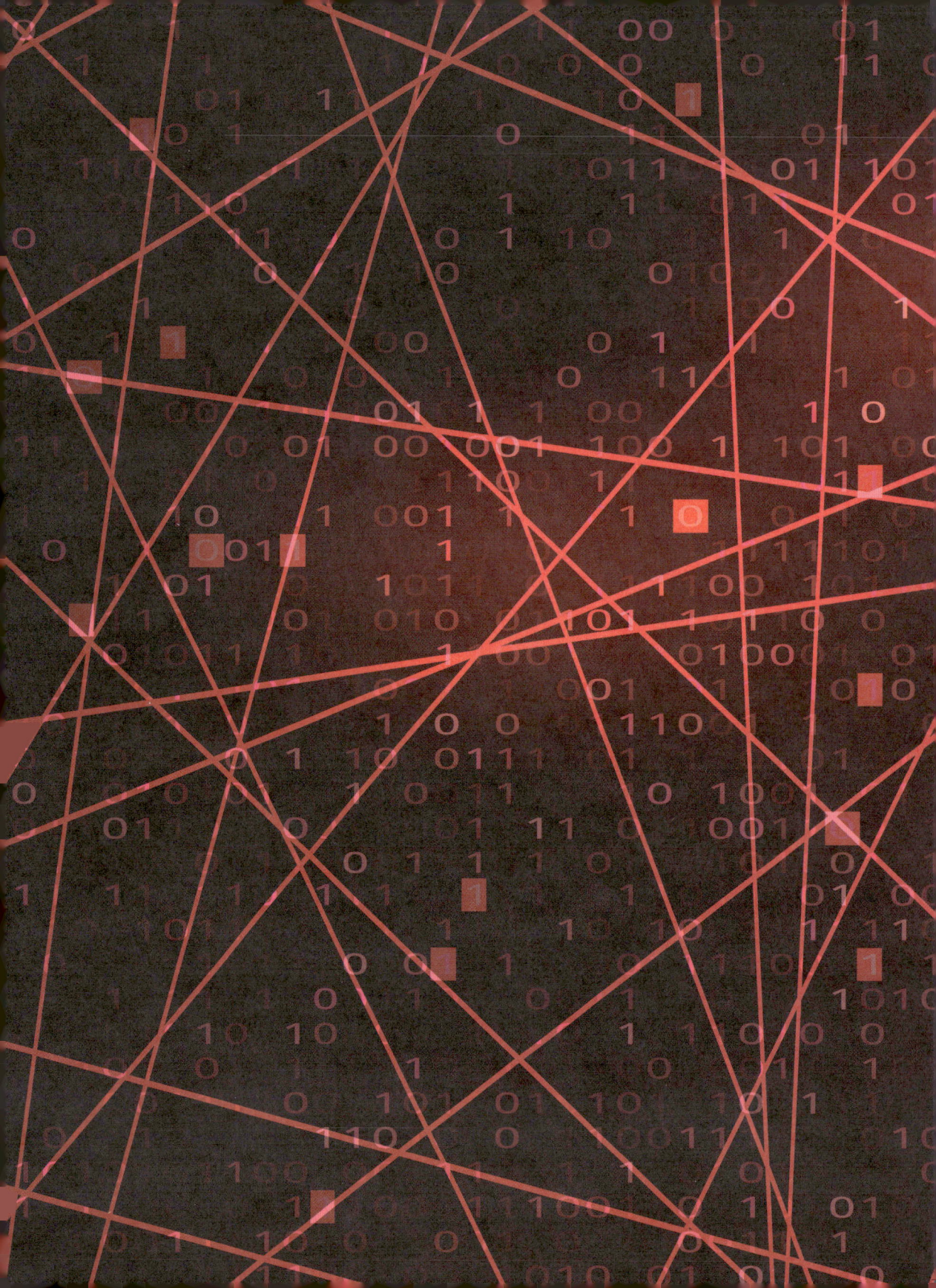